Maria

A True Story of Faith and Forgiveness

Auschwitz Survivor

Maria Gascon

Maria

A True Story of Faith & Forgiveness
AUSCHWITZ SURVIVOR

as told to Mary J. Steinkamp, S.N.J.M.

Guardian
B O O K S

Belleville, Ontario, Canada

MARIA – A TRUE STORY OF FAITH & FORGIVENESS
Copyright © 2008, Mary Steinkamp

Library and Archives Canada Cataloguing in Publication

Steinkamp, Mary J. (Mary Julia), 1931-
    Maria : a true story of faith and forgiveness / Mary J.
Steinkamp.

ISBN 978-1-55452-243-9

    1. Gascon, Maria. 2. Auschwitz (Concentration camp). 3.
Prisoners of
war--Poland--Biography. 4. Catholics--Poland--Biography. 5.
World War,
1939-1945--Prisoners and prisons, German. I. Title.

D805.5.A96S75 2007   940.54'7243092   C2007-907278-X

For more information or
to order additional copies, please contact:

Sister Mary J. Steinkamp
2014 NE 19th Ave
Portland, OR 97212
or
Maria Gasson
3125 NE 23rd Ave.
Portland, OR 97212
Phone: (503) 288-0548

Guardian Books is an imprint of *Essence Publishing,* a Christian Book Publisher dedicated to furthering the work of Christ through the written word. For more information, contact:
20 Hanna Court, Belleville, Ontario, Canada K8P 5J2
Phone: 1-800-238-6376 • Fax: (613) 962-3055
E-mail: info@essence-publishing.com
Web site: www.essence-publishing.com

I dedicate this book to:
God, the Father,
Jesus, my Beloved,
God, the Holy Spirit, who has guided me from my child-
hood to this day and still guides me every day of my life,
and to my heavenly Mother Mary who is always helping
me. I thank Jesus and Mary for all the blessings in my life,
and I pray that they will guide the children of today.

Table of Contents

Preface

In October, 2006 when Maria asked me seriously about writing her life story I told her I had to make a holy hour in presence of Blessed Sacrament about it first. I did that at Holy Rosary Church on October 12, 2006. I prayed for light and wisdom. At that time this is what I felt Jesus was saying to me:

"O my child,
Beloved worry-wort,
Put the book and the publishing in my hands. I desire it and I will see it through. My thoughts are not your thoughts. Trust Me. Look to Me and live. Live today in the fullness of my love. Do not be concerned about tomorrow for I hold all your tomorrows in the palm of my hand. Maria's story will help people know Me and my love.

Your job, beloved worry-wort, is to trust me and write. Write of My love, My hope, My strength. Let the world see forgiveness; let them see the true meaning of the cross. Do not get hung up on details. Let Mary B. help you with the business end. She is my most capable servant. I wish to be glorified in

this book. You are the channel. Be a peaceful one. OK?
Remember no fear, only trust. Trust it all to me with all your
heart for I will see it through. I ask Maria to be my witness,
my little handmaiden. I was with her at Auschwitz; I won't let
her down now. And your job is to be a channel of my love, my
peace, my hope in a very torn world.
Shalom."

The book is finished. I am grateful. For me it was a prayer, a sign of hope, a way to say "Thank you, God" for people like Maria who make this world a better place, for people who are morally strong enough to stand up for truth no matter what.

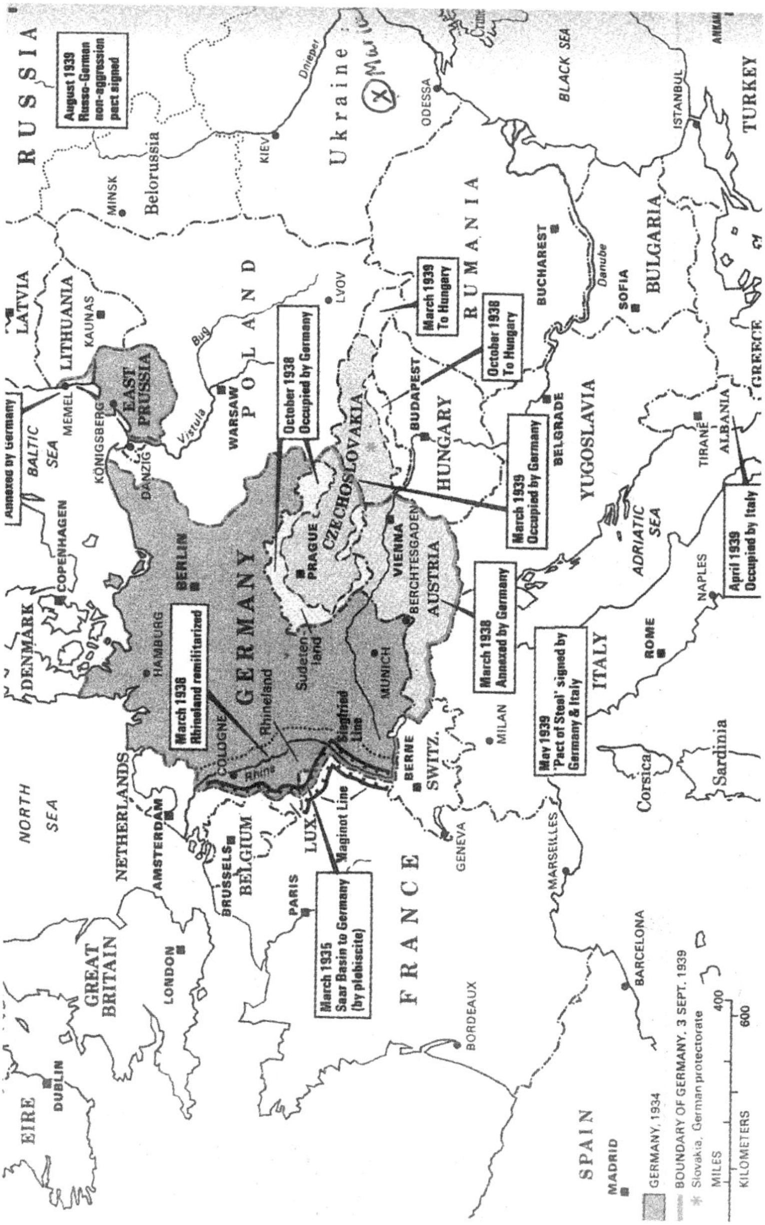
August 1939 Russo-German non-aggression pact signed
Annexed by Germany
March 1935 Saar Basin to Germany (by plebiscite)
March 1936 Rhineland remilitarized
March 1938 Annexed by Germany
October 1938 Occupied by Germany
October 1938 To Hungary
March 1939 To Hungary
March 1939 Occupied by Germany
May 1939 'Pact of Steel' signed by Germany & Italy
April 1939 Occupied by Italy
GERMANY, 1934
BOUNDARY OF GERMANY, 3 SEPT. 1939
Slovakia, German protectorate
MILES
KILOMETERS

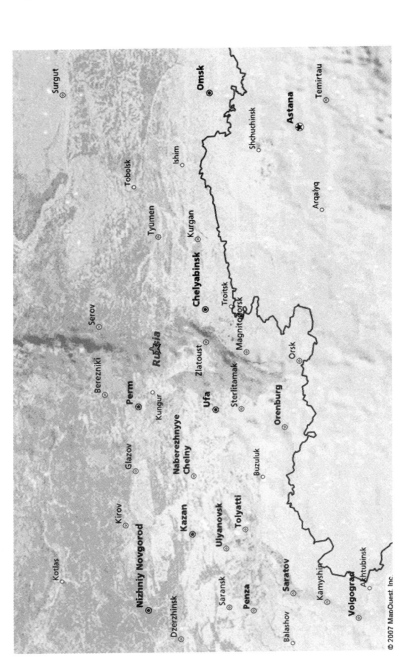

Surgut

Omsk

Temirtau

Astana

Shchuchinsk

Ishim

Tobolsk

Arqalyq

Tyumen

Kurgan

Chelyabinsk

Troitsk

Serov

Magnitogorsk

Russia

Berezniki

Zlatoust

Orsk

Perm

Kungur

Ufa

Sterlitamak

Orenburg

Naberezhnyye
Chelny

Glazov

Buzuluk

Kirov

Kazan

Ulyanovsk

Tolyatti

Nizhniy Novgorod

Kotlas

Saransk

Penza

Saratov

Kamyshin

Dzerzhinsk

Volgograd

Akhtubinsk

Balashov

© 2007 MapQuest, Inc.

Chapter 1

My Papa, Gone Forever

I, Maria Haluschkewych, was born in 1928 in Poland of Polish parents. A short time later my parents moved to the Ukraine in white Russia near a small village named Rudina about 150 miles from the Black area (see map). I was a blonde, blue-eyed, smiling baby. I loved to laugh and later dance and sing. My father was a tall, six-foot two-inch, good looking man. My mother was about five foot five and very beautiful. My three brothers and I and my father's parents lived in a big wooden house. It was beautiful and spacious, with my grandparents in their own section separated from us by a long hall. Beautiful weeping willow trees, lofty maples, and plentiful birch trees surrounded our house. Marigolds, petunias, and fragrant roses added to its beauty, as well as many lilac bushes, where my oldest brother, Greg, would later hide and secretly read his books on God. My other grandparents had a house and farm across the river.

We lived on a 200-acre farm with many woodlots, hills, and ponds. Many birch, pine, and some fir trees were plentiful in the woods. In the spring, the birch trees wept and we collected the juice and drank it. It was very tasty. We even saved some for winter.

I made friends with a neighborhood girl, and we played together on the farm. One summer day, we decided to get some berries. Beyond the barn in one of the woodlots, there was a hillside that they said had berries, so we went to look. As we went down the hillside, we came to a sand pit full of nice soft yellow sand, kind to our bare feet. (We ran barefoot all summer.) We hadn't gone far when we disturbed a nest of black snakes that hissed. I was terrified and screamed, "Run!" We didn't stop running until we were sure there were no snakes near us. We never returned to play in that sand pit. We did find some luscious blackberries, though, and ate our fill. After we got back to the house, we never told anyone about the snakes and we always avoided that spot.

There was much to do on the farm because we had many animals. I loved all the farm animals: pigs, chickens, geese, ducks, cows, sheep, and horses. I had a cat I called "Kitty." She was fun to play with. I was very fond of the geese, which I talked to every day as I took them to the pond. Helping them, I learned to swim at an early age. When I was about six, I did many farm chores, such as feeding the chickens and gathering the eggs. I learned that I could carefully open the end of an egg and drink it from the shell. So every day I took one egg for me. It was fun slurping it up. As long as I was healthy, my parents didn't fuss about what I ate, so I ate more from the source than from the table. I was crazy about crunchy carrots fresh from the ground and big juicy apples right off the tree. Milk from the cow was best.

Apple harvest was a busy time but a fun time. Everyone pitched in to pick the apples and carefully store them in the cellars. Then we had a big dance and celebration outside. My brothers played the accordion and harmonica. Everyone danced. Papa was very good at it, and my mother would dance as light as a feather, smiling all the time. I sang a lot. I learned many songs as a small child and loved to sing.

Sometimes my brothers and I got into a little mischief, like the time Papa had sixty loaves of bread for his farm workers and we took one and climbed a big tree and sat up there and ate it. It was jolly fun watching them below looking for that loaf. We didn't get caught. Another time, when I didn't feel like eating my breakfast of pancakes and oatmeal, I waited until my mother was facing the stove, then I hastily opened the window and let Red, my dear horse, gobble up my breakfast. (The pasture went up to the window on that side of the house.) My mother turned back to the table and said, "My, you ate fast!" I agreed and took off to play with my friend.

Another time, my brothers and I ate our neighbor's poppy seed. It was delicious. We thoroughly enjoyed it until the neighbor reported us to Mom. We heard the report and hid under the bed. My mother made us come out. Somehow she knew we were under there. And we got in trouble.

My father raised a large patch of garden peas each year, probably a full acre. I loved eating them right off the vine, and I would go sit in the middle of the patch and eat. No one could see me. I sat there laughing as I heard them calling my name. It was jolly fun.

Horses provided the power on the farm, pulling the plows, cultivators, mowers, and other farm machinery, as well as pulling sleds and buggies. My father had three stallions for riding. I was very thrilled the day he taught me to ride. Papa rode Blackie, and I rode Red. I loved the smell of the leather harness and saddle and the fresh scent of new hay in the horse stables. The feel of the wind whistling by my ears and my long blonde hair streaming out behind gave me a wonderful feeling of freedom. I have many fond memories of my dear papa. I was not fond of getting up in the morning, but he would call me and then tickle my chin to get me awake. I always had a big smile for my beloved papa.

I remember the day Papa gave me a piglet to raise. I named him Pinky. First I carried him around, and then when he got bigger, he followed me like a pet dog. I remember on summer days lying on the warm grass with Pinky beside me. We would nap back to back. Pinky was a faithful friend. He grew big and strong but was still my loyal companion. It was a sad day when Grandpa butchered him. But food was important, and Grandpa was a practical farmer.

In the winter, Clydesdale horses would be used to pull a big sleigh at Christmas time. We would go caroling in a group. I loved those outings. I loved any chance to sing, and this was it. People would shower us with treats, cookies, bread, sausage, and drinks. When we had more than we could use, we gave it freely to poor neighbors. Papa did the same with produce. He shared potatoes, currants, wheat, bread, apples, pears, and honey with the village people.

My maternal grandparents lived on a farm across the river, so sometimes I helped at their place. I loved helping my grandmother there, who cared for little children, like a daycare. When I was six, I met a neighbor family who had a lot of children, including Nicholas, a boy of six years, who could not talk or walk. He was very thin and frail. I asked his mother if I could take him to our goose pond where I swam. She said, "Yes," so I would put him on my back pig-gyback-style and haul him down there daily. He was small and skinny. I was quite sturdy, so it was not difficult. I would put him in the water and rub his arms and legs and teach him how to swim. After three weeks of what might be called warm-water therapy, I got him to walk a little, and by six weeks he could talk. I loved little children and wanted so badly to help that it was just natural that he should respond. Today I still enjoy little children immensely.

An unforgettable day occurred in March, 1937, when I was nine years old. I was at school with two of my brothers, Alex and Vasca, when the principal rushed to our class-room and said, "Hurry home quickly!" We ran all the way. When we got there, the secret police were taking my father away. They had him handcuffed and in a sled where they had other handcuffed men from the village. My mother was crying. I cried. My brothers looked on helplessly as big men dragged him away.

That was the day I met communism. The farm was no longer ours. It was now part of the people's collective for everyone to share. Our papa was gone. I would never see him again. I would never hear his hearty laugh or feel him swing me up on his strong shoulders. Gone forever. I stood there in a daze and then put my arms around my mother and cried into her blouse. She held me close. All three brothers hugged her and said, "Mama, we will stand by you. Don't be afraid."

Two months later, my mother took a train to the labor camp to see him and was told that he was dead. That night I cried myself to sleep. I was filled with memories of all my father had been to me. I went frequently to the pasture where Red and Blackie had been and sat on the fence and cried for my papa. Then we moved to a one-room house in the village. I was sent to live with my grandmother across the river. My brothers and mother shared the one-room house in the village. Greg died of pneumonia the next winter. Mother was sent to work on a community farm. Life would never be the same with Papa gone forever.

Chapter 2

My Mama, Almost Gone

After the communists took our farm away, we moved to a little house in the village. It had only one room. My three brothers and mother slept there, and I stayed with my grandmother. There I got to talk to the geese and bring them bread. They had work horses, cows, chickens, and ducks. I still had my beloved Kitty. My grandmother would make vern cakes. These are made with grated potatoes, eggs, and a little salt. Then cottage cheese is put in the middle and sealed in and then they are fried. Mmm! Delicious! She also made kasha, which is made from cooked millet, eggs, sugar, butter, and evaporated milk and is then baked. These were two of my favorite dishes.

God was never mentioned, and no prayers were ever said aloud for fear of being taken away. My mother had to work on a community farm. The rations she brought home were small and inadequate. I remember my brothers going hungry at her house. Greg had some books on God. He read them secretly and never ever told anyone or discussed them, for fear of being taken away. He tried for a math job in another city. He was very smart. He died there at eighteen of pneumonia.

Maria's younger brother, Vasca, about 12 years old.

Maria's brother, Alex, about 16.

Later I found his books and read them. I found the "Our Father" prayer in one of these books and learned it. I prayed it! It was great. My heart sang. I was about eleven years old. A whole new world was opening up for me. That night I had a marvelous dream. Jesus and Mary were standing there with their hearts open to me. They took my heart and gave me their hearts. I felt the power and love of God in me in a new way. I began praying every day for the souls of my father and Greg who had died.

In 1939, the churches in Russia were opened. The ban was off. We could attend. We could pray out loud. God was with us. We moved to a city and were just twenty blocks from a Greek Orthodox church.

Before we moved to the city, I crept out at 6:30 in the morning to walk six miles to the church on Sunday. It took me several hours. Mass was at 10 a.m. and finished at 1 p.m. It was beautiful walking to church. Birds were singing. My heart was racing. The air smelled fresh, of new-mown hay. I sang, I jumped. I skipped all the way to church. The service was glorious. I knew in my heart that Jesus was truly with me. I loved every minute of it. I sang my way home after the services and arrived late in the afternoon. After my mother knew where I was she didn't worry about me. For an eight-year-old I was quite independent. Sometimes a girlfriend went with me. But if she couldn't I went by myself.

My mother asked for an explanation but was not unhappy. She reminded me that I must tell her next time so she wouldn't worry. "You know, anything can happen to little girls out by themselves." I was happy that my mother was so understanding. I felt God was very important in my life. Many things, including a number of dreams, led me in this direction. This next one was powerful.

It was a very significant dream. I was in a big river with yellow sand on the bottom. There was a crucifix there. I could see it on the yellow sand. I tried to grab it. I couldn't get it, although I tried three times. Each time, an ugly black snake tried to bite me. I felt awful. Jesus wanted me to have that cross. The next day, that crucifix was on my little table. I made a place for it with fragrant red roses from the garden. These dreams helped me. I was never afraid; I knew God and Mary were with me in a very powerful way. "Thank You, Jesus!" Another time, the Blessed Mother woke me up so I could get to church. I talked to God and His mother a lot. I called her Mom.

How Maria saw cross.

I felt that God was helping me with the terrible sorrow of losing my dear papa. He was gone forever from this earth, but he would be in heaven waiting for me with his hearty laugh and big smile. Every day I prayed. My mom took me to church the first time, and after that I went with others or by myself. We walked probably four kilometers. Mass was at 10:00, followed by a break at 12:00 for lunch and then an afternoon Mass. I went to both and walked home rather late. I remember those walks. The birds were chirping, and there were many squirrels chattering in the trees. It was a wonderful walk. I talked to Jesus all the way. When my friend and I sat down to eat our lunch outside the church, there was a little mound of fresh dirt. It was so warm and nice, so we sat on it and ate.

Once there was a homemade bomb in the church, but we didn't know it. It never went off during the services. It exploded that night around 10:00 and caused no damage except for knocking a picture off the wall.

In 1939, many Jews were sent to a neighboring city and

many others were shot right in our village. We were made to watch these brutal slayings. Some were shot but not dead. After the massacre, they were buried and the ones that weren't dead were struggling to come out of the dirt, all bloody. We were forced to watch so we would know what would happen to us if we didn't obey. I would say to God as we were forced to watch, "I forgive on the spot. You take care of it. It is more than I can do." There were some German soldiers who refused to do these brutal slayings, and they were shot or sometimes sent to the gas chambers with the Jews. Other times they tied people to trees, forced us to watch, and skinned them alive while they screamed in pain. Their bloody bodies were then thrown on the ground where they finally died from loss of blood, and the skins were used to make purses and lampshades for their wives.

If a German soldier was killed in the village, the German soldiers gathered the rest of the villagers together and put them in a barn, locked it, and set it on fire. My grandmother's sister, who was forty at the time, was in that barn. She managed to get out through the smoke and run to our house some three kilometers away. She was badly burned. Her hair was all gone. Her clothes were burned off. She told us what happened and dropped dead right in front of us. I sobbed and asked the Blessed Mother to help us. Another thing the soldiers did was to round up the men of the village, put them on a wagon, gather the village people to watch, and then shoot the men. It was very brutal and sad.

In 1941, when I was thirteen years old, the Czechoslovakian soldiers had me and a friend work in the kitchen. They had a lot of sweets we prepared for the German soldiers. I got sick from eating too many. The soldier in charge was nice and let me take home sugar and flour for my mother. One time, a Hungarian soldier caught us on the way home and made us wash clothes for him and his bunch. We giggled a lot and washed the clothes, and then before we hung them up, we dropped them in the dirt. They got so stiff no one could wear them. He never caught us again.

Every Sunday, I went to church. Even when my friends begged me to go to a party I said, "Church first, then party." They understood. We had some wonderful parties with dancing, singing, and playing musical instruments such as the guitar, which I played.

One stormy day, when the thunder was rolling and lightning was flashing, the Germans and Russians were fighting over our village. It was terrible. We stayed inside, hoping not to die. I went to bed, and the guns were still booming. I prayed the "Our Father" prayer over and over and went to sleep. I dreamed I saw the Blessed Mother. She stood in the doorway. She was dressed completely in white. I jumped out of bed, knelt before her, put my head on her feet, and prayed the "Our Father." I woke up and saw the sun streaming in. The wind had died down. It was calm, peaceful, not even a branch was moving on the big trees. The Russians had taken the village back. I had only twenty-five minutes to get to church. I hurried. I got there in time to sing with the choir, which I loved to do.

Several months later, I had a powerful dream. Our Lady appeared dressed in black in the backyard. I knew something bad was about to happen. Mary was helping me get ready. That day we were ordered by the soldiers onto a cattle freight train. My friend Yara and I were put in a freight car by ourselves. We were taken to Poland to work in the wheat fields. The Germans needed the grain. We were there about four months.

One day we saw the soldiers beat and drag away my mom because she refused to go off to another city to work in the hospital for wounded soldiers. They ripped her clothes and made her bloody from beating. We didn't know where they took her. We couldn't find our mom anywhere. My two brothers and I sat down and cried.

Later, we were standing in the courtyard for roll call. I stood in the front line. All of a sudden, I felt pushed forward. I turned and ran into the building where my friend Nadia lived. The Gestapo were close behind. "Quick, make the bed and hide me in it." Her face turned pale. She ran to do it. I hid under a fluffy goose-down comforter and scarcely breathed. I kept praying, "Mary, keep me safe." Two Gestapo searched very thoroughly. They ran a bayonet into the bed three inches from me.

I started breathing again when they left the room. Nadia said, "Maria, don't ever do that to me again. I was scared stiff."

"I'm sorry. Thank you for helping me."

I went out a different door and met a colonel in the street. He had a big whip hanging from his belt. He greeted me, "Hello, Fraulein, I need someone to work in the kitchen."

I replied, "Okay, I'll take the job." I worked in that house several days with Olga.

Later I went to a house across the courtyard from us with swinging doors and saw my mom. She called, "Maria!" I didn't answer because I had learned she was in the death dungeon. Those locked up there were taken out every Monday and shot. I had worked three days with Olga in the kitchen. I told her where my mom was. I kept praying, "Mary, save my mom."

That Sunday, I went to Mass across the street and after Mass stayed and prayed in front of a big statue of Mary that was down on the floor. "Mary, save my mom."

I confided in my friend my problem. She said, "The colonel is sleeping now. We will fix his favorite lunch and you bring it to him and ask for your mom's release."

She fixed frog legs and crab, and I brought it to him. I said, "Herr, please release my mother. How would you feel if it happened to you this way? I know you have a good heart. I know you are a good man. Please." I looked at him and prayed quietly.

He looked at me, rubbed his chin, and said, "Fraulein, she should be shot. She disobeyed." I kept praying. He added, "I'm going to do what I can."

I replied, "Danke schoen," did my best curtsy, and left. That evening, the colonel released my mom. I give all the credit to the Blessed Virgin. I take no credit. I thanked Jesus and Mary the rest of that day.

While I was still working there, another officer asked me to help him. He took me out to the woods. I kept praying; I was afraid. I realized he wanted to rape me. I said, "No! You'll have to kill me. And then you will have that on your soul for the rest of your life." He looked at me, frowned, and then he turned abruptly and said, "Let's get back." I never saw him again. We were shipped out a few days later. I thanked Mary for saving me.

Chapter 3

Camps

We were ordered by the soldiers onto a cattle freight train. Most of the people were stuffed into the cars like sardines, but my girlfriend Yara and I were put into a car with a German officer. It was cold wooden car with straw on the floor and narrow slats through which one could see out. Perhaps it was because we both spoke German. He called us swine, but Yara and I were not inhibited by him, although we were careful not to sass him because if you did you were whipped unmercifully. We giggled a lot and laughed. We had good food; the others only had bread and water. We had cheese, bread with margarine, lunch meat, and clean water. I can't explain why. We had a bucket in the corner of the car for a bathroom. It was a very primitive system. I do know I did a lot of praying.

We were taken over the Volga River to Austria. The prisoner car was sent ahead of a train carrying about forty wounded German soldiers so that when it crossed the bridge over the Volga, if there were any booby traps or bombs, the soldiers wouldn't get blown up. The Volga River was wide and a very dark blue. We got safely across, but the soldier train was blown up and they were killed either by the blast or the river. Many were too wounded to swim. We could hear their frantic screams. I prayed for them: "Jesus help us all." Then I prayed the "Our Father." It was my most special prayer. We spent about a week in Austria.

We were taken by trucks to Auschwitz. We had very little to eat, one piece of bread and one cup of fake coffee for breakfast and a turnip or turnip soup for supper, no lunch. We were confined to the trucks while they had long lines of Jews going into the showers. There are many smells in the world, beautiful ones like lilacs in the spring on the farm and vile odors like a rotten potato. On the farm, there was an occasional skunk, and of course, farms have smelly manure piles. I had smelled many things, but I could not identify the odor at Auschwitz. I didn't know what the awful stench was, but it continued night and day. It was like the odor of decay, but it had chemical overtones, like a strong cleanser. It was nauseating, especially when the wind was blowing in our direction. They played beautiful music, The Blue Danube and other pieces by Strauss, as all this went on. After two weeks of literally living on the trucks, we were

Auschwitz pictures taken in 1970 by Elaine and Noel Higgins. *Used with permission.*

lined up for the showers when the soldiers broke into our lines and took us away. We missed going in by two hours.

Empty gas cans used in gas chambers.

Execution wall where prisoners were shot.
Tourists leave flowers.

Next we were taken to a camp in Eichen-Felden, which was a work camp. We were about twenty people. We did farm work: gardening, weeding, and picking fruit, especially apples. We had to rise promptly at 6:00 and work until 6:00 at night. There was no lunch. We lasted there six months. The menu was still bread and turnips. To this day, I never eat turnips—I pass them by. My clothes were falling apart. We could wear clothes from the piles in the camp from the Jews, but I couldn't handle that, so I just wore my own. I had a blue dress with a pink flowered vest and a long black coat. It was frayed and ragged on the bottom. The sleeves were torn. My coat was hanging in tatters, but I still couldn't bear to part with it. My toes were sticking out of my shoes. It was a bit chilly.

While we were still in Poland, my brother Alex caught typhoid. He was very sick. For two weeks, my friend and I fed him water and a little food in small bites and prayed a lot. He got over it. God heard our prayer. Many died of TB and typhoid. "Thank you, Jesus, for healing Alex." His darling wife, Eva, was pregnant, so we were all happy to have Alex alive.

Next we were taken to Camp Stutthof, or Hof for short, a concentration work camp where I was to spend the next two years. It was surrounded by a high barbed fence with plenty of electricity. I stayed away from it. The wooden barracks had lice- and flea-infested straw to sleep on. It was chilly, around twenty degrees in the winter.

Eva's baby, Nina, was born in Hof. She was a darling little girl. We showered lots of love on her and marveled that she didn't die from the scanty food supply. God took care of us. We prayed more than we ate, and somehow He sustained us. The beds of straw in the Hof camp were full of lice. I was lucky, because a German lady who owned a barn nearby let me sleep there in her clean haymow. She even gave me a goose-down quilt, which was warm. Her German boss approved. Our heads were shaved in an attempt to cut down the lice population. My beautiful blonde hair, which reached my waist, was gone. I looked like a zombie with all the other zombies. They put DDT on us to stop the lice. I still shudder when I think of that smelly, lice-infested place.

The adults worked on rebuilding blown-up railroads. Part of the time, I worked as an interpreter for the German railroad boss. I could speak German. I got yelled at by both sides. I did the best I could, but it was tricky. The workers had to clear away the debris and put down new metal rails and wooden ties. It was heavy and hard work.

I also worked on the farm and unpacking goods from the trains with the other children. We put the goods into trucks for shipment. Some of the goods were cookies and chocolates from the US that were sent for the prisoners, who never got them. The Germans ate them. As we transferred them from train cars to trucks, we had one person stand guard and then we opened one box of cookies and took turns eating them. We carefully buried the empty box and never got caught or we would have been shot or whipped.

As we walked back from the apple orchards where we picked the fruit, we would pass thirty or forty dying people by the roadside, where they were left to die, mostly from starvation. When they were too weak to work, they were just left there. Their eyes would be begging us for food, but we couldn't help them or even offer sympathy or we would get shot. I remember vividly the eyes of one starving man. I longed to help him, but I couldn't so I went to my bunkhouse and cried and prayed.

At night, I told fairy stories to the children until they went to sleep. I begged God to blot out of my memory the terrible screams of those from the death dungeon in Poland and in the camps where they were flogged. I said to God, "A demon has gotten into them. Please, God, get him out. Jesus, come into the hearts of these people the way You have come into my heart. Set them free. Please."

Chapter 4

Camp Hof

Everyone at Camp Stutthof was starving. There I met a Jewish lady of about thirty, who was really starving badly. She could hardly walk. Her bones were sticking out. She begged me for food. Her gaunt face and shiny skin told me the final stages of starvation were setting in. I managed to get a half a loaf of bread, which I tried to surreptitiously get through the barbed fence separating us. She was in the next barracks. The wires were far enough apart that I could slip it through. I had waited until dark, but some prisoners were watching and they knocked her down and took it away. She stumbled back to her barracks. I saw her the next day. She was black and blue, with bloody gashes on her arms. Two days later she died. I sat down and cried, "Dear God, it is so hard to forgive. Please help me, and let Rosa help me from heaven. Jesus, You are my hope. Be with me." I felt very sad, but peace came over me and I slept. Somehow I knew that God would get us through all these atrocities.

I can still hear the screams of Jewish babies and young children who were used alive in experiments. This was done in a compound about a block away from where were stationed. I was given the job of making the parents watch and not turn their heads away when their children were being cut up alive. I saw with my own eyes children as young as six months and as old as twelve being cut open and their hearts and livers taken out. Two people would hold the child down, and the doctor would take a sharp scalpel and thrust it into the chest and pull out a live heart. It was the most inhuman act I have ever witnessed. Their screams live in my memory. I still feel cold all over when I think of it. And I pray that God will help me.

The worst one was a child being cut up with the parents forced to watch. Their only crime was that they were born Jews. "Jesus," I prayed as I turned away and got sick to my stomach, "help me. This is too much. How can anyone do this to another human being?" Then I very quietly slipped out so I wouldn't see any more, trusting no one would catch me for not doing my job. I got outside without fainting, but my knees felt weak. I sat down on the grass and prayed some more. "Help me, God. You alone can handle this." Carefully I made my way back to the work area. I realized the Gestapo wanted us to see what would happen to us if we didn't obey *schnell* (quickly). I prayed and prayed, but there was no peace.

Camp Hof was near a railroad station, a woods, a lake, and farmland. It is about 150 miles from Munich and not too far from Berlin. It surpassed many camps in lice-infested prisoners suffering from malnutrition, typhoid, TB, anemia, and all sorts of skin rashes.

The German foreman whose job it was to get the railroad rebuilt had me for an interpreter. I did my best to translate his German into Polish and sometimes got screamed at by both sides. The Polish resented me having a better job, and the officer was frustrated because it took so long. *"Arbeite schnell"* seemed to be his motto ("work quickly"). But the guy liked me because he often gave me half a meat sandwich and said, "Don't let anyone see this." I was careful not to. I would eat one bite and give the rest to my mom. It was tricky. I managed not to get mugged. My mother was extremely grateful. She would give me a big hug and say, "Maria, you are my savior."

We worked from 6:00 am until 6:00 pm. Even when the Gestapo ran out of real work, they invented work for us like digging holes and filling them in. *"Arbeit macht freesen"* was the sign over Auschwitz: "Work makes you free." And if a prisoner refused to do this hole-digging stupidity, he or she was shot on the spot. It was a very upside-down world I lived in for four miserable years, but I never lost hope that somehow God would get me out of it. I was at Camp Stutthof, Hof for short, for two years and in the other camps and detention places for the other two years.

In the spring of 1945, American bomber planes flew overhead. The Americans were pushing the Germans back to Berlin. There were three long trains of German soldiers going to safety, but they were a target for the bombers. We were outside working on the railroad. It was in horrible need of repair. Bombs began to fall. It was horrible. People were dying all around me. I couldn't breathe. I kept gasping for breath and finally ran toward the bridge. I had no shoes. They had fallen off. My right foot stepped on a fallen German soldier. He was still warm. I can still feel his chest in my foot. I kept running. Then I blacked out. When I came to, I was lying flat on my back on the other side of the lake. How I got there I couldn't say. I was covered with soot and dirt from head to toe. I looked like a chimney sweep. I stood up and discovered nothing was broken or cut. Truly a miracle. Dead and dying were all over. Bloody hands reached for help. They screamed, cried, and moaned. I shuddered, "God, help them." I was in no shape to help them.

Probably 1000 Polish prisoners and German soldiers died in that bombing. The living had to put their mangled bodies on trucks to be hauled away. It was a gruesome task. I helped pick up a ten-year-old boy whose face was bloody and whose legs were badly broken. I prayed and tried not to get sick to my stomach. My mom and my sister-in-law and baby Nina were safe in the barracks.

The sirens would scream, and we would have to run to the underground dungeon. It was there that I met a man with a ball and chain on his leg. He had been wearing it for six months. Anyone caught stealing food got this ball-and-chain treatment. They were forced to work lugging it around. In this camp, the officers cut it off deciding he would stay put. At last he was free. We waited in the dungeon for a long time while bombers screamed overhead. The chain man couldn't wait any longer, so he went up to see what was going on. He was promptly shot. Would this nightmare ever end?

Chapter 5

Americans Come

After the bombs fell and I narrowly escaped death, I ran to where my mom and sister-in-law and baby Nina were. They were all safe. They were so happy to see me they hugged me despite the grime. I was black from head to toe.

I looked for my closest friends, Greg and Zosa. They were gone. I would never see them again. Witty Zosa with her sparkling blue eyes and giggling laughter was no longer on this planet. I cried and prayed some more.

I remembered the discussion I had with my German foreman when the planes few overhead the first time at 11:45. I said, "Those are not German planes."

He insisted, "Yes, they are." *"Du bist dumkopf."* ("You are a dumbbell.")

"Nein, das kann nicht stimmen," I replied. "No, it cannot be right. They have a different sound than German planes." Then at 12:10, they came back and dropped bombs. This railroad station was a crucial spot. They had located it and returned. I can still hear the "Shhhaaahhh" sound the bombs made just before they exploded.

The Germans needed the railroad. We had to put it

back together. It was a grueling task. First clear the debris, then install new ties and new metal rails, making sure everything was carefully done so the trains would travel safe. The German foreman still had me translating. I prayed a lot even on the job and set aside half an hour in the morning and half an hour in the evening to pray.

Two weeks later, the American soldiers came in. We were grateful. We cheered. We sang. We thanked God while tears were streaming down our faces. Our long exile was ended. Two years of hell in this camp was going to be over.

A train car with lots of packages of food was sitting there. "Go take whatever you want," the Americans told us. My mom sent me to get some. I followed the crowd. They pushed. They shoved. They climbed over each other. Some yelled obscenities if anyone got in their way. It was a mad rush. I couldn't do that. "Jesus help me." I turned around and went back.

On the way I found some new material, beautiful cloth in autumn hues, rich oranges and swirling golden browns. I picked it up and took it back. My mother said, "Maria, did you get anything?"

"No, Mama, too many people pushing and climbing over each other. It was like mad animals snarling and biting. I couldn't do it. I can't act that way even though I am hungry."

My mother replied, "I go. You stay." She came back with big chocolate bars, flour, oil, and baking soda. The next day she managed to make bread. Her bread was so good. I ate two big chocolate bars that day and got sick, violently sick.

The Germans were gone and so were the turnips. We had no regrets. The American soldiers fed us their rations and told us to go where we wanted and do what we wanted. Freedom was never so sweet. My mother decided on Augsburg, some 150 miles away. They gave us free passes, and we went by train. It was a lovely train, no cattle cars, no corner bucket for a bathroom, no soldier pointing a gun at us. We laughed. We sang. We prayed. We hoped to find our brothers. But they were gone forever, and we never ever found any trace of Alex and Vasca. May they rest in peace.

In Augsburg, we had a summer place or big camp with two spacious rooms, which I shared with my mother, my sister-in-law, Eva, her baby, Nina, and her sister. It was peaceful and nice, no bombs, no beating, no cutting up people for experiments, no one yelling *"schnell,"* no sobbing at night, no starving, no tramp, tramp, tramp of those dreaded Gestapo boots, no lice, and best of all, no turnips! I cannot face a turnip. In the store, I pass them by and I thank God for all the good food we have, but most of all I thank Him for freedom.

While we were there, my mother found a lady to sew me a dress from the pretty material. It felt good to be rid of the rags and to have shoes on my feet.

1946 after concentration camp. Maria's mother, niece Nina (born in concentration camp) and Maria.

(Maria's brother, Alex, and Eva were Nina's parents. Alex never saw Nina. He was killed in another camp.)

Summer barracks in Augsburg, Germany, where Maria and her family lived after the war.

Maria at Ausburg, before she met her husband.

Nina, at high school graduation– Maria's brother Alex's daughter who was born in the concentration camp.

The Americans were very good to us. They set up a Red Cross station where we could go to dances and have coffee and doughnuts. It was fun to do the Ukrainian dances that we knew. There was strict curfew at 9:00. My girlfriend and I wanted to go see the town one night, so we crawled under a barbed wire fence. There was a nice big hole someone had conveniently dug. An American soldier on duty caught us and took us to the headquarters. We had to stay there all night. They gave us beds, but we didn't sleep. We talked and laughed and giggled so much the officer probably thought we were crazy. We spoke German, so he could not tell what we were saying. In the morning, he took us back to our house. We didn't try to see the town again at night. We were told it was dangerous to be out.

I had an American friend who took photographs around the city. He took me with him. It was fun to see the various sights. He was a good man. My mother trusted me to be with him. One day, as we were walking along the street, we meet two American soldiers. They were very friendly. I didn't know that one of these would be my future husband. He asked me where I lived. I told him. He came to see me. Twice I slammed the door in his face and didn't let him in. "Maria, why did you do that?" my mother asked me.

"I don't want to see him." The third time around he asked me to go to the dance at the Red Cross. I loved to dance. It was fun with Herbert. He was a staff sergeant in the army and a smooth dancer. We got acquainted over the next few months. Since the war ended in April, Herbert didn't have to go fight but he had to stay on and do occupation force duty. He had to patrol in the daytime and just come home to sleep at night. It was a wonderful summer.

Maria, second from left, in national Ukraine dance group.

U.S. Army— Herbert, future husband and friend. Herbert is on right.

Chapter 6

Wedding Bells

We both enjoyed the Red Cross dances. I had danced since I was a little child. Dancing was second nature to me. It was as natural as breathing. Herbert was a very smooth dancer and clearly enjoyed it also. He tried to learn German so we could communicate. But we did very well without words. Augsburg has many roses, and Herbert loved to bring me gorgeous bouquets.

One day he brought me a pint of ice cream and said, "Eat it right now." I did not understand. I put it carefully under my bed. I had never eaten ice cream, and we had no refrigerator. It melted and made a big mess. He laughed long and hard about that. *"Verstenhen sie?"* ("Do you under-stand")

"Nein" I replied, for I had not understood. We had many good times during the summer whenever he could get off duty. We explored the city. We walked. We talked. We admired flowers and the beautiful green hills surrounding the city. In December, I discovered that I loved him. One evening he brought some late flowers, chrysanthemums, and proposed. He knelt on one knee and said, "Maria, *ich*

liebe dich. I love you. Will you be my wife?" I looked into his beautiful brown eyes and said, *"Ya, ich liebe."* I felt that God had brought us together.

Maria and Herbert, courting days.

Now it looked like my dream might come true. I had dreamed of someday going to America.

January 14th is the Russian New Year. It is a time of big celebration. Herbert said to me, "Let's get married on the 14th." I agreed heartily. We planned the wedding. We kept it simple. We asked the Russian bishop who was in Augsburg with us and said Mass if he would do the ceremony. He agreed.

Somehow Herbert got two simple rings, very plain bands, and I borrowed a beautiful dress and veil from a friend. Eva was my maid of honor, and Herbert had a soldier friend for best man. The dress had gorgeous lace on the hem and sleeves, and the veil had a crown of roses.

As we walked into the large hall that served as a church, people lined our pathway three deep on either side for 500 yards. It was a very festive occasion. The big dinner afterwards was a potluck where everyone brought something. We couldn't have our honeymoon then because Herbert had to go back on duty in Munich. I stayed in Augsburg until April when Herbert found me an apartment in Munich. It was lovely being closer. I was in Munich from April until June, 1946. My mom and Eva stayed in Augsburg.

Maria and Herbert, Jan. 14, 1946.
Married by Orthodox bishop.

Herbert and Maria. She is wearing a coat she made from Herbert's army bathrobe.

Then Herbert made arrangements for me to go to the US. First I had to spend two weeks in France. I didn't manage to speak that language. It was nothing like Polish or German or even English! We went on a war brides' train and then on a special officer's ship named *Cristobal*. It was first class. We could watch movies. I saw *Yolanda* with Fred Astaire. Then I got seasick and was in bad shape for seven days. They fed me oranges and orange juice. It didn't help. To this day I avoid oranges. They are not quite as bad as turnips but pretty close.

My friend and I both had miscarriages on the ship. When we got off, we were both put in the army hospital in New York for two weeks. When we got over that, my friend Nadia and I both went exploring in New York. It was lovely; there was no curfew.

We bought lots of food: meat, milk, bread, fruit. It was so wonderful to see so much! We stood there and exclaimed, "Look! Look at all this food! I have never seen so much! Thank you God!" We ate some of it but some went to waste because two young women could not eat that much. I was very careful after that never to let any food go to waste. I remembered how it felt to be hungry all the time. And in America, I never ever forgot to thank God for every meal. I can see the pleading eyes of that man left by the roadside in the camp to die of starvation. It was the Gestapo technique, when the workers were so starved they couldn't move, to put them by the roadside and let them die—no more water, no more food. And the grass within their reach had all been pulled off and eaten. One poor fellow tried eating the earth. It didn't sustain him.

Next I took the train to Walla Walla to live with Herbert's family until he got back. I arrived in July. Herbert came home in October. They lived in a nice home on two acres outside the city. Herbert's mom worked in the cannery for sixty-five cents an hour. She got me a job there too.

Herbert built a house 500 feet away for us on property from his dad. We had two bedrooms. Our four children were born in Walla Walla. Herbert, the oldest, was born in July. I had twenty-four hours of labor with him. Then after I got home I got a terrible kidney infection. I was unconscious. Father came and anointed me. They thought I was going to die. But after he anointed me, I opened my eyes and I saw Jesus walk out of the room with Father. I got well. God was with me. Our son Alex came next. We spent a few happy years in Walla Walla and then moved for a short time to Baltimore. Our third son, Danny, and our darling daughter Nina were born in Walla Walla also, after our stay in Baltimore.

Chapter 7

𝕷ife in the 𝖀𝖘

I worked in the cannery and set aside $500 so I could get my mother transportation across the ocean. It was wonderful having her safe in the US. She came by ship and landed in New York. From there she took the train to Walla Walla and lived with us for about four years.

Then my husband joined the army again and we had to move to Baltimore He was two years there at an army base. In Baltimore, my mom met a fine man at a Russian Orthodox church. They were happily married and settled in Baltimore. He was a widower and had six grown children. One had been a pilot and was killed in WWII in Germany. He never got over the loss.

In Baltimore, I worked as a cocktail waitress. We had two children at that time. My job went from 6:00 pm until 2:00 am. When Herbert got home at 5:00, I had dinner ready, and he took care of the boys and fixed breakfast for all of us at 2:00 am He fried potatoes, poached eggs, and made toast and coffee. He went to work at 6:00. We went to sleep.

The apartment where we stayed had cockroaches. I couldn't stand them. The neighbor lady said she just brushed them off and ate the food. I couldn't do that, and I couldn't sleep with them crawling around. I left the lights on. They didn't come out in light. I lost twenty pounds in the three months we lived there. Then we moved closer to where Herbert worked so that he could walk to work.

When we lived at that first apartment, I had to drive home in terrible fog. It was so dense I had to stop the car to see if I was still on the road, and sometimes it took four hours to get home. The second apartment was much better. There were no cockroaches. But his job was bad. The army cut his pay, and we had a hard time getting enough food. We fed the children first, and then if there was any left, I ate. Herbert ate at the base camp. At Christmas, there was only one can of Campbell's soup and a few soda crackers. I went out in the yard and found a branch and put it in a canister to make a little decoration. I found the canister in the garbage bin. Luckily our children were too little to know about Christmas, so they didn't feel left out.

After two years in Baltimore, my husband quit the army and we went back to Walla Walla. We drove from Maryland in three-and-a-half days. We took turns driving. Money was so short, we had borrowed $100 from my mom. We drank coffee to stay awake and took turns driving. We often went ninety miles an hour. When we got within twenty miles of home, we were too tired to go any farther, so we stopped at a farm and asked if we could sleep in their barn in the hay. The farm couple obliged, and we slept twenty-four hours straight. We had only $20 left when we got home.

All our four children were born in Walla Walla. Herbert was oldest, Alex was next, Danny was third, and Nina was last. My husband got a job driving a truck hauling huge rocks. I worked at a local drive-in restaurant. One day two young cops came in and called me "Chick." I thought they were ordering chicken, so I brought them a large chicken sandwich. They were surprised but paid for it. They never called me "Chick" again. Later I learned what "Chick" meant.

Maria, Greg, Alex, Herbert, Danny

Greg (son), Danny (son), Nina riding Daddy Herbert, Alex

In January 1971, we celebrated our twenty-fifth wedding anniversary. It was a happy day. Our children fixed a very nice party with many friend and neighbors. It was like a giant potluck, with roasted turkey, salads, cake, and coffee. There were about 150 people attending. We took time to thank God for many blessings.

In November that same year, Herbert was planning a trip to Bend, Oregon. Our son Alex, who also drove a truck said, "Dad don't go. Get your truck checked first. There is something wrong with the engine. I can tell by the way it sounds."

"Knock it off and don't be a worry wart. It will be just fine."

"Okay, I'll follow in the other truck." That is what Alex did. They were just outside Bend, when Herbert's truck went berserk and hit a big tree. Alex went as fast as he could to get help. There was a house nearby, but no one was home. The paramedics came and took Herbert by ambulance to the hospital, but he died before they reached the hospital. Alex called home. I was not there, I was at work. He got his youngest brother Danny, who wrote me a note and took off for Bend.

I thought back to the night before Herbert left for Bend. I had dreamed about Mary. She stood by my window completely dressed in black. My own father came to me in that dream and laid down beside me. He too was dressed in black. I knew something bad was coming. So I begged Herbert not to go, but he brushed me off, just as he had done to Alex. It was a sad day, November 22, 1971. Life would never be the same. Alex was so completely devastated that he didn't talk for three months.

We moved to a house across from the school and

church on 23rd Avenue. It was in a sorry condition. The doors were practically falling off. Everything needed fixing. I had to hire a man to get the place livable. In fact, that house was in such bad repair it sold for $10,500. I prayed a lot and held down three jobs to make ends meet. One day I said to God, "This is too much: I can't do it." And God said, "Yes, you can." I did it.

Alex was still in high school at Washington High. They were playing baseball, and he got hit by a bat on the base of his skull. The school sent him to Damasch Hospital. There they gave him the wrong medicine, and he became a mental patient. I did not know how to get the proper help.

Maria's son Alex, about 14.

I had a tough time paying bills, medical and the others. But I never gave up; I kept praying and asking God to help me. This was difficult but it was much better than the concentration camps.

Nina by her truck

Christina, granddaughter at 10 years old, now 32

Tamara, great-granddaughter about 4 years old, now 15

Chapter 8

Family Life

My oldest son, Herbert, was married before my husband was killed in that fatal truck accident. He lived in an apartment and worked as a restaurant manager. He and his wife had four children.

Alex, my second oldest, was not well and lived at home.

Danny, my youngest son, was in the army for several years and then became an engineer and worked on airplane parts and landing gear. Later he had a job in Beaverton working with cell phones. He married and had three boys and one girl.

My daughter, Nina, married, and both she and her husband were truck drivers. They had one girl, Christina, who I took care of through her early years.

I now have nine grandchildren and six great-grandchildren.

I worked hard to make ends meet, holding down three jobs simultaneously. The first one was a receptionist for a rock company. They sold fancy rocks that people used to make decorative walls and fences. I would come home from this job and drink some strong coffee, take a hot shower, then work from 5:00 pm until 11:00 pm as a cocktail waitress. I would sleep from 12:00 until 4:00 am, go to church, and then take Christina to the babysitter. It was a difficult schedule.

Once I caught pneumonia, but I kept working. I prayed hard and told God how painful it was. Then at church I saw the thorns from Christ's head floating by. Somehow I knew that Jesus was helping me be patient with my situation. When I got home, I made some hot chicken-noodle soup and slept. Amazingly, I felt much better, but it took two weeks before I was completely well. God helped me through this hard time.

I loved all the little children, and they loved me. Tamara said, "My grandma is my whole world." They are so innocent and beautiful. I can see why Jesus said, "Let the little children come to me." Tamara is very gifted in singing and acting. She is a natural actor and will stage a play at the drop of a hat. I took care of her until she was ten.

After ten years of truck driving, Christiana, Tamara's mother, had a nasty accident on bridge back east. She was driving a semi and turned incorrectly. She ended up hanging off the bridge, unable to get out. The police came and got a huge crane to rescue her. It was her lucky day that she wasn't killed. She decided to end her truck-driving career.

As a family, we still get together for holidays: Easter, Christmas, Fourth of July, Thanksgiving. I enjoy hiding the Easter eggs all over the house and yard so that the little ones need to take two hours to find all of them.

"Look Grandma, I found one with money!" Nicholas shouts, rattling a plastic one with a few coins inside. I pray that God will always watch over my family and keep them close to Him. I have much to be thankful for.

I look back on my life and am most grateful for all the times God has saved my life. I talk to Him like I would my mom and papa. I keep falling, but He always picks me up. He is closer to me than my jugular vein. His love and goodness have followed me all the days of my life, and I would like to say in closing, "Children, love and respect your parents. Parents, always respect your children and bring them up to know and love Jesus. If you have God in your life, all the other pieces will fall into place."

At age seventy-nine, I look back over the years. Seventy years ago I lost my dear father. After age nine, I never saw him again, yet I know he is in heaven smiling down on me and I will see him again. My mother is with him. She was lucky to survive the Nazi camps and come to America. I am grateful to be a US citizen. This country has some problems, but they are small compared to Gestapo violence and Bolshevik dominance.

I am alive. I am free to go to church. No one shoots me for praying. I may receive the Eucharist. I can walk right in. I don't have to sneak past an armed soldier. It is such a grace to be free to worship God. The Eucharist is the high point of my day. Truly Jesus is my Daily Bread. I thank Him and His beautiful Mother, and I thank God for my blessings.

I believe that God is with us and if we keep praying, all will be well. The prayer that is my favorite is the "Our Father." It has been powerful all through many dangers. One devout "Our Father" can pull a person out of a complete disaster. I have seen it. I tell no lies. God has been and is with me. I pray that He is with you too.

Painting: Mother of the Unborn

MOTHER OF THE UNBORN

Miss Tidwell, an American artist, was inspired to paint this beautiful depiction of our Blessed Mother grieving over the millions of aborted babies. Normally, a picture like this would take her months to finish. She completed this one in two hours.

The stars around Mary's head represent the crown of the Woman of the Apocalypse (Revelation 12:1): "A great portent appeared in heaven, a woman clothed with the sun, with the moon under her feet, and on her head a crown of twelve stars." The large star is the "Star of Bethlehem." The rose colored ball in the lower left corner symbolizes the earth in turmoil. The glow of Mary's heart is an evident sign of her tremendous love for all her children, especially the most helpless of all.

The incessant weeping over this horrendous evil has blackened her lovely eyes. The baby's Guardian Angel seems to be both saddened over the death of his charge and grateful for the Blessed Mother's care and concern.

The baby bears the five wounds of our Precious Saviour. Both baby and Angel are weeping and the baby's hands are clasped in prayer.

The reason the Blessed Mother's hand and fingernails are dirty is that she has to scoop and dig out these precious babies from trash bins, garbage dumps, and as in Wichita, Kansas, from a pile ready to be burned with dead animals at their dog pound.

Give Children Life

I have always had a very special love for children, especially very young ones. I have been very saddened by abortion in our country. I pray daily for parents and children, for mutual respect that children will obey and that parents will always cherish their children at all ages. I pray that our country and the world will put an end to abortion. I can still hear the screams of the children in the Nazi death camps as many children not yet dead were thrown into the piles of corpses and left to die.

I want to share this picture of the Mother of the Unborn in an attempt to help people respect and love the unborn.

May God bless all of you who have since 1973 so bravely fought for the lives of these little ones. May the Author of Life bring you new hope that some day as a country we will respect life. To care for the least is to care for life.

Maria, a True Story of Faith and Forgiveness as told to:

Mary J. Steinkamp, SNJM
2014 NE 19th Ave.
Portland, OR 97212
Phone (503) 281-3449
e-mail
steinkamp@hevanet.com